How to Smoke in Public Without Being Seen

First published in 2006 by HEADLINE PUBLISHING GROUP

ISBN 978 0 7553 1613 7

Cataloguing in Publication Data is available from the British Library

Designed and typeset by The Flying Fish Studios Ltd
Printed and bound in Great Britain by Bath Press

Headline's policy is to use papers that are natural, renewable and recyclable products and made from wood
grown in sustainable forests. The logging and manufacturing processes are expected to conform to the
environmental regulations of the country of origin.

HEADLINE PUBLISHING GROUP
A division of Hodder Headline
338 Euston Road, London NW1 3BH

www.headline.co.uk   www.hodderheadline.com

How to Smoke in Public Without Being Seen

Robert Jebb and Damien Weighill

headline

Hide your fag in your fist.
Cough.
Have a drag as you cover
your mouth.

Slide your fag inside a Biro.
Suck as you chew.

Get a job
supplying smoke machines
for eighties-style discos.

Travel by time machine back to the fifties, when everyone smoked. Expensive, but you can always sell the patent.

Submit a piece of modern art to the Tate.

RIDICULE AND
EXCLUSION
by Sharon Corper

Train as a balloon modeller.
Fill your art with smoke.
Allow it to deflate,
and enjoy a drag while
entertaining those pesky kids.

Sit on a fag.
And clench.
Two ... Three.

18

Allow your life to go off the rails and spend most of your time in a soup kitchen. Have a brown paper bag for your super strength lager, and a smaller version for your fag.

Go for a Guinness World Record.

21

Read a clever book.
People will be too intimidated
to argue with you.

Work in a fancy dress shop.
Wear a (non-flammable)
chicken suit and smoke
all day long.

25

Learn the oboe.
Join the woodwind section
of an orchestra.

Referee as many basketball matches as you can. Have two whistles. One to blow and one to suck.

Join a darts team.
Take your time when aiming.

Join a health club. Get a tan.

33

Disguise your tabs
as breadsticks.
Nibble daintily, suck furiously.

Do a degree in sports science.
Modify the spirometer
so that it's connected to 20
of your favourite smokes.

Wear a hoodie to the office.

Get a job in a phone box.

41

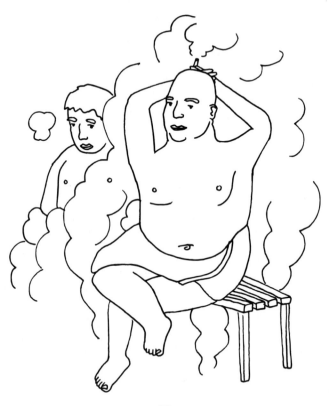

42

Spend time in a steam room.

Become a chef.
Burn everything.

45

Put on a Noel Coward play.
Everyone smokes all
the way through.
Even the children.

Adapt a plug-in air freshener
to emit bursts
of fragrant tobacco.

49

Become a mad professor.

Join a look-alikes agency.

53

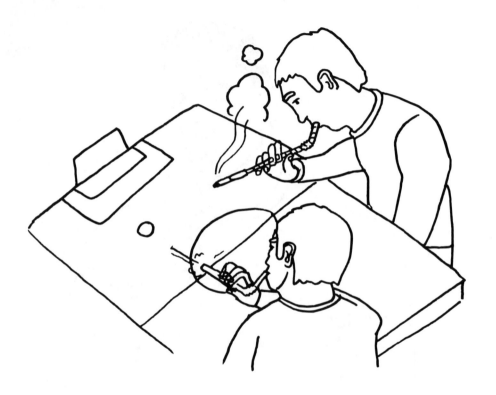

Enter a blow football league.
Don't expect to win much.

Become a Star Wars fan.
Attend conventions.

57

Develop asthma.
Convert your inhaler.

Become a surgeon.

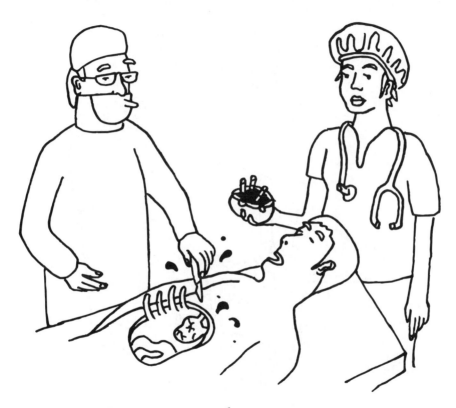

Sweep chimneys.
No ashtray required.

Test a new snorkel.
Above sea level.

65

Be the front end of
a pantomime horse.
Seasonal smokers only.

Go to confession.

69

Smoke via Mr Snippit, your ventriloquist's dummy.

Take your dog to the pub. Tell everyone you've taught it to smoke. Have a few puffs to get him started.

74

Pretend to be Mexican.

Become a mechanic.

77

Create a diversion.

Robert Jebb was born in Shropshire in 1971 and was educated at Glenalmond College, Perthshire. He worked as a copywriter in most London advertising agencies, which he didn't like much, before starting his own agency, which he likes a lot. He lives in Oxfordshire with his wife Shazza, son George and shivering whippet Millie Bum Bums.

Damien Weighill was born in Hartlepool and attended Northumbria University where he excelled at colouring without going over the lines. He lives in London, where he works as a graphic designer and freelance illustrator.